Prancing Pony

THIS EDITION
Produced for DK by WonderLab Group LLC
Jennifer Emmett, Erica Green, Kate Hale, *Founders*

Editor Maya Myers; **Photography Editor** Kelley Miller; **Managing Editor** Rachel Houghton;
Designers Project Design Company; **Researcher** Michelle Harris; **Copy Editor** Lori Merritt;
Indexer Connie Binder; **Proofreader** Susan K. Hom; **Series Reading Specialist** Dr. Jennifer Albro

First American Edition, 2025
Published in the United States by DK Publishing, a division of Penguin Random House LLC
1745 Broadway, 20th Floor, New York, NY 10019

Design copyright © Dorling Kindersley Limited 2025
Text and Illustration copyright © WonderLab Group LLC 2025
24 25 26 27 10 9 8 7 6 5 4 3 2 1
001-345518-April/2025

All rights reserved.
Without limiting the rights under the copyright reserved above, no part of this publication may be reproduced, stored in or introduced into a retrieval system, or transmitted, in any form, or by any means (electronic, mechanical, photocopying, recording, or otherwise), without the prior written permission of the copyright owner.
Published in Great Britain by Dorling Kindersley Limited

A catalog record for this book is available from the Library of Congress.
HC ISBN: 978-0-5939-6594-8
PB ISBN: 978-0-5939-6593-1

DK books are available at special discounts when purchased in bulk for sales promotions, premiums, fund-raising, or educational use. For details, contact:
DK Publishing Special Markets, 1745 Broadway, 20th Floor, New York, NY 10019
SpecialSales@dk.com

Printed and bound in China
Super Readers Lexile® levels 500L to 610L
Lexile® is the registered trademark of MetaMetrics, Inc. Copyright © 2024 MetaMetrics, Inc. All rights reserved.

The publisher would like to thank the following for their kind permission to reproduce their images:
a=above; c=center; b=below; l=left; r=right; t=top; b/g=background

Alamy Stock Photo: Trinity Mirror / Mirrorpix 23b; **Dreamstime.com:** Accept001 21tr, Anjajuli 19cr, Astusia 6-7, Baibaz 27cr, 27crb, Nigel Baker 11t, Victoriia Baliura 20bl, Sucharat Chounyoo 29b, Steve Cole 14t, Elenapashinnaya 19cra, Fotoschab 8-9b, Sopan Hadi 21tc, Nynke Van Holten 8tr, Maria Itina 9b, Jevtic 29tr, Microvone 5cb, MitaStockImages 3c, Naschysillydog 22tl, Evgenii Naumov 13cb, Pikepicture 6ca, Brinja Schmidt 17tr, Elena Schweitzer 9tr, Stacey Steinberg 16-17tr, Wally Stemberger 12-13, Tartilastock 8cr, 9cra, Zuzana Tillerová 26, Tribalium 28cl, Kseniya Abramova / Tristana 1, Yehor Vlasenko 12tc, Ivonne Wierink 24-25; **Getty Images:** AFP / Ina Fassbender 24clb, Hamish Blair 24cra, The Washington Post 25c; **Getty Images / iStock:** Evgeniya_Mokeeva 1cl, 3cb, 4cra, 13tl; **naturepl.com:** Kristel Richard 13cr, Carol Walker 15b; **Shutterstock.com:** Nishad Ashraf 24cr, Clara3434 21cr, JW.photography31 4-5

Cover images: *Front:* **vendor: Dreamstime.com:** Josieelias; *Back:* **Dreamstime.com:** Bigmouse108 cl, Topgeek cra; *Spine:* **Dreamstime.com:** Josieelias

www.dk.com

This book was made with Forest Stewardship Council™ certified paper – one small step in DK's commitment to a sustainable future.
Learn more at www.dk.com/uk/information/sustainability

Level 2

Prancing Pony

Becky Baines

Mwah!

Contents

6	Just Horsin' Around
10	The Mane Event
14	Haaay, Neighhhbor!
18	That's Horse Sense
22	More Horsepower
26	Giddyup!

28 Stable Manners
30 Glossary
31 Index
32 Quiz

Just Horsin' Around

What's that prancing playfully in the pasture?

It's a pony!

All the fun of a horse in a pint-sized package! Ponies are seriously cute critters.

Ponies

- Short and stocky
- Thicker coat
- Can survive on little food
- Stubborn
- Smaller hooves
- Shorter stride—about three human steps

Are you my mother?

Lend a Hand

Horses and ponies are measured in hands. One hand is about four inches (10 cm)—about the width of a human hand! Ponies usually measure under 14.2 hands. Anything above that is a horse.

Horses

- Long and lean
- Thinner coat
- Need lots of food to survive
- Less stubborn
- Larger hooves
- Longer stride—about four human steps

The Mane Event

Ponies have been around for a very long time. Experts think they first came from a breed of wild horse. These horses didn't grow as big because there wasn't enough food to eat.

Meanwhile, humans needed help with hauling and transportation. They needed help around the farm. The smaller horses made excellent helpers. They were strong and easier to take care of than bigger horses.

I'm a real wild child!

People began to train these horses and keep them as pets. The horses had babies, and those babies had babies. They got even smaller and less wild. Ponies were born!

As ponies spread across the world, their bodies adapted to suit their environments. They became better at the tasks they had to do. Different kinds of ponies got good at different things. Today, there are over 200 different pony breeds!

Haaay, Neighhhhbor!

I think it's pasture bedtime!

In the wild, ponies live in a herd. In a pony herd, there are rules to follow. Each herd has stallions, mares, colts, and fillies.

mare
adult female

stallion
adult male

colt
young male

filly
young female

Each herd has a leader. The oldest mare is usually the leader. The head stallion's job is to protect the pack. Every other pony falls in line somewhere behind them. There's a first, second, and third in charge, right down to the very last pony.

When colts are a few years old, they leave their herd. They form their own herds. Fillies usually stay with their parents' herd.

Mares carry their babies for almost a full year. When foals are born, they hit the ground running!

Within half an hour of entering the world, a foal can stand. It drinks its mom's milk.

What a beauti-foal sight!

Within two hours, it's prancing along with the pack!

This quick ability to move on their own is all about survival. Since ponies are prey to wild predators, it's important for foals to be able to make a quick getaway.

That's Horse Sense

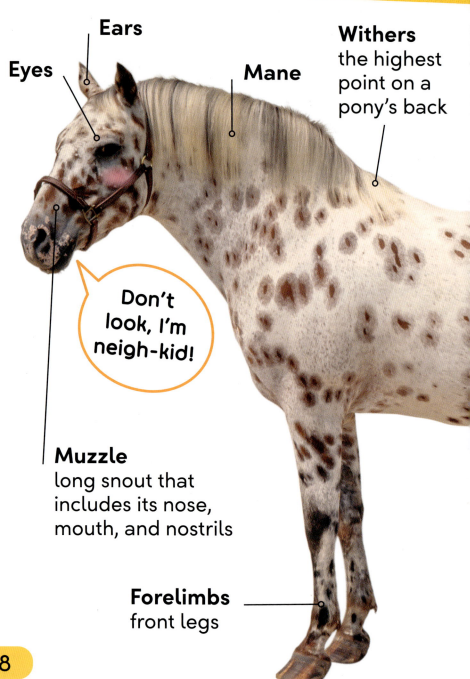

Eyes

Ears

Mane

Withers the highest point on a pony's back

Don't look, I'm neigh-kid!

Muzzle long snout that includes its nose, mouth, and nostrils

Forelimbs front legs

Get to know your pony!

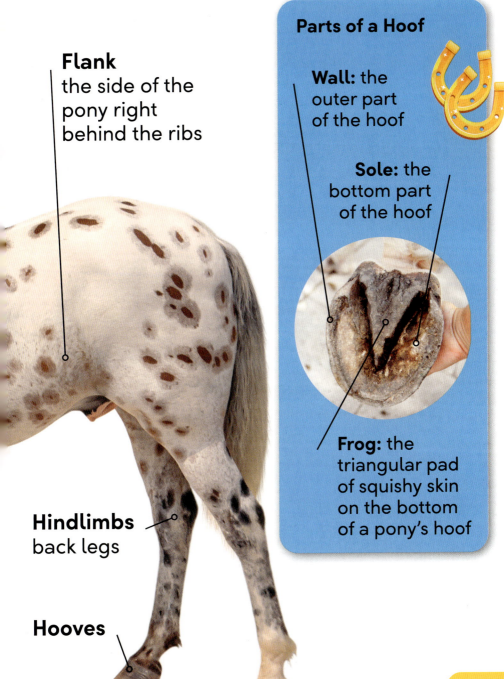

Flank the side of the pony right behind the ribs

Hindlimbs back legs

Hooves

Parts of a Hoof

Wall: the outer part of the hoof

Sole: the bottom part of the hoof

Frog: the triangular pad of squishy skin on the bottom of a pony's hoof

19

Vision

Ponies' eyes are on the sides of their faces. They can see movement almost all the way around them all the time. But the position of their eyes and their long muzzles also means they have blind spots. Don't approach a pony from directly behind. It could get spooked and kick.

I'm a real sense-ation!

Hearing

Pony hearing is all in the movement of the ears! Each ear has 10 muscles, so the pony can rotate their ears in many directions. This helps them locate and identify sound, and make it louder.

Sense of Smell

Ponies have powerful sniffers! Wild ponies survive on plants and grasses. They need to sniff out what's okay to eat and what's not.

More Horsepower

Ponies have been human helpers from the very start. Their strong and sturdy bodies are just right for carrying and pulling heavy loads.

Since ancient times, people have ridden horses and ponies. They used the animals to take them places that were too far to reach on foot.

If they needed to bring the family, they'd pile everyone into a horse-drawn carriage. Two horses could pull up to 14 people at a time. But if they only needed to haul a few people or a small load, pony carts did the job just fine. Many people still use pony carts today.

Wanna race?

This is some serious pony-power.

Penny the pony pulling a full wagon, 1950

Today, ponies have lots of important jobs!

Companion Pony
Horses training for big races are known to keep a pony friend on the sidelines so they don't get lonely.

Emotional Support Pony
Ponies make great support companions for people who suffer from a number of medical problems. They can help their owners overcome health issues.

Therapy Pony

Ponies make great friends for people in need of a little fuzzy affection! Connecting with animals can be healing, so some organizations will bring ponies to care homes or even hospitals to visit. Pony muzzle nuzzles go a long way toward making people feel better.

Changing the world one human at a time!

That will be 400 carrots.

Giddyup!

Fast Facts

- Ponies may be small, but they are strong!

- In the wild, ponies are able to survive on little food.

- Ponies cannot breathe through their mouths.

- Ponies can get sunburned.

- Ponies love sweet flavors. Sour or bitter? Not so much.

- The world's smallest pony is only about 20 inches (51 cm) tall.

- Ponies get lonely without a friend.

Stable Manners

If you meet a pony, good stable manners will help you become BFFs in no time!

- **Always say hello.** Never sneak up on a horse. Speak softly but clearly. Offer your flat hand. If it touches its nose to your hand, it is interested in getting to know you!

- **Make sure the pony can see you.** Never approach from behind. Remember: ponies kick!

- **Mind your brush.** If you are grooming a pony, stand off to the side, never directly in front or behind.

- **If you are saddling or mounting a pony,** make sure you have the guidance of a professional.

- **Watch your feet.** Ponies can't see down, so they don't know where they are stepping.

Glossary

Adapt
To change behavior or physical features to become successful in an environment

Breed
A type of horse with a similar size, appearance, and behavior

Companion
A person or animal that keeps someone company

Environment
Physical surroundings

Foal
A baby pony or horse

Mount
To climb up to ride

Predator
An animal that hunts other animals

Prey
An animal that is hunted by another animal

Saddle
To put a saddle, or a seat for a human, on a horse

Survival
Continuing to live in the face of difficult circumstances

Therapy
Treatment that heals a person physically or emotionally

Index

breeds 11–13
Chincoteague pony 12
colts 14–15
companion pony 24
Connemara pony 13
ears 18, 21
emotional support pony 24
eyes 18, 20
fast facts 27

fillies 14–15
foals 16–17
hearing 21
helping humans 10–11, 22–25
herd 14–15
hooves 19
horses 8, 9, 22–23, 24
Konik pony 13
mares 14–16
parts of a pony 18–19
pony features 8

predators 17
senses 20–21
Shetland pony 12
size 8
smell, sense of 21
stable manners 28–29
stallions 14–15
therapy pony 25
Timor pony 13
vision 20

Quiz

Answer the questions to see what you have learned. Check your answers in the key below.

1. What unit of measurement is used to measure ponies and horses?
2. What does a pony do if you approach from its blind spot?
3. What do you call the highest point on a pony's back?
4. What is a baby pony called?
5. True or False: Ponies are sturdy and strong.

1. Hands 2. It kicks 3. Withers 4. Foal 5. True